I0462377

Get It Done:
93 Real Tips and Tricks For Momprenuers
(and Moms and Business Owners Everywhere)

By Kathy Catlin Davis

DEDICATION

For John and Kaden for inspiring me to be the best me
I can be, and for Jim for sharing and supporting our
vision for our family.

ACKNOWLEDGMENTS

This book would not be possible without the support of my mother, Jolien Catlin, and without the advice, thoughts and opinions shared by the contributors: Natalie Rose, Jessica Brockway, Susan Young and Sheryl Matthys.

INTRODUCTION

My name is Kathy Davis. I'm a wife, a mother, and a business owner. From the outside, I'm pretty sure most people think I have always led a charmed existence. But, like many people, I have a back story.

Going way back in history, I grew up as the oldest of four children in a comfortable middle class suburban life. There was no discussion on whether I would go to college – it was much more focused on which one I would attend. I knew from a small age that my career choices needed to be focused on security – and that my dreams would need to be put to the side so I could do something practical.

Fast forward a decade or two. I graduated from college and law school. I married a charming young man and I went to work in a law firm. Wow! I had made it.

But checking off the boxes of the American dream wasn't enough for me. After four unhappy years of marriage, my first husband and I divorced. A year later, my father died suddenly at his desk. A few months after that, my mother was diagnosed with breast cancer.

What a lot of stuff to hit you all at once. It definitely felt like you couldn't even move past one thing before another one hit you. I felt like it was all I could do just to hang on.

I plugged away at the life I had created – the job, the suburban home. I even dated and eventually married a wonderful man.

But one dark night I had a blinding realization that I was allowing myself to just go through the motions. I was still waiting for permission to follow my own dreams.

That night I started writing again, after more than a decade away. Less than a year later, I had several books published, a regular blog and I was freer. A year after that, I left corporate life and opened my own business, helping other entrepreneurs start and grown their businesses.

What did you want to be when you grew up? Do you remember? I do. First I wanted to be a writer. Then I wanted to be a lawyer. Ironically enough, now I do both of those things. But I'm not going to sit here and tell you that my life came together effortlessly.

As we grow up, it is easy to let life derail us from our dreams. Our relationships, the things that happen in our individual worlds and the world at large all shape who we are, who we become and what we do with the bits and pieces that make us each unique.

How do we find our big ideas? How do we take the "I want to be a firefighter" when we are little and turn it into starting a foundation dedicated to supporting people hurt in house fires?

Do You Have A Dream Board?

A dream board is a simple and painless way to keep that which is important to you front and center in your life.

Set up a bulletin board in your office, room, kitchen, or other place where you frequently think. When you see a picture of something that inspires you, post it on the board. Keep this up for a few weeks. See where it leads you.

You can also do this by creating boards on Pinterest. If you don't want to share your private thoughts and dreams, Pinterest does let you create secret boards.

However you choose to create your dream board though, make sure its something you look at frequently. On Pinterest, it can be easy to create it and then let it sit out there in cyberspace. If the board is up in your kitchen, it is much more in-your-face and hard to ignore.

Your dream board will guide you to a few things,

without you trying too hard…. Your real dreams.

Creation

Koestler in the Art of Creation stated that the creative act is not an act of creation in the sense of the Old Testament. It does not create something out of nothing. It uncovers, selects, re-shuffles and combines already existing facts, ideas, and skills. The more familiar the parts, the more striking the whole.

What do you want to create?

I think sometimes in our society we are given two very clear options. You can either be a stay at home mom or you can work for a living and you are portrayed if you are someone who works and someone who does not care as much about your children. There are always some people who will attempt to portray you as bad.

And I think the very interesting thing, not just from Susan's perspective but from many of the mom's perspectives, is that women with small children who own their own business are looking at multiple realities. They are looking at the reality that they do have to do something to pull in income for their families, that they have economic responsibility in their household. They are utilizing their talents and their gifts. They are utilizing things that they spent years going to school to develop, gifts and talents that they have strengthened over the years through looking for other people and volunteer work and they are wanting to utilize those and give back to the world. They want to support other small businesses and other companies and helping them grow as well which overall just strengthens our economy. And at the same time they are loving their children and they are wanting enough time to be with those children and to raise those children to be good citizens in our society.

And so part of our message in this book is not just look at all these tips, but also you can work, you can have a company, you can have a business and you can still be a great mom. It is figuring out how to balance and juggle all the balls and keep them in the air without beating yourself up because one of them might have fallen.

Juggling our roles

As women, we juggle the roles we have in our lives – mom, wife, sister, daughter, chef, housekeeper, carpool driver, business owner, employee, family bookkeeper, chief nutritionist, keeper of the schedule.

Sometimes it can be overwhelming – especially when our schedules start to feel like a game of Tetris. And sometimes, we know there's a whole somewhere, where things aren't quite fitting together and as much as we try to fill the void, we know there is something more.

I think we can also let our roles define us – to the point that changes are scary. I've recently started climbing out of the box marked "attorney." I'm changing gears. I'm building a whole new spot where

I can show all sides of who I am – the attorney, yes, but also the small business adviser, the consultant, the writer. I would be lying if I didn't say that it was a little bit scary. How many of you are holding back on something because you're scared?

But one thing I've learned over the years is that life is short – and never as long as we think it should be. We should tell people we love them. We should enjoy the moment. And we definitely shouldn't wait to follow our dreams, because we never know how much time we have.

What are you juggling today?

93 REAL TIPS AND TRICKS FOR MOMPRENUERS (AND MOMS AND BUSINESS OWNERS EVERYWHERE)

1. **Know what is important to you.** For me, my family is my top priority – being able to interact in a quality way, being able to financially support our household, and taking care of my health to improve my chances of being around for the long haul. This is my big "why," and the pieces and parts that everything else I do ties back to – from morning workouts, to goals in my business.

2. **Don't Multitask.** This may seem like bad advice. How else can you get everything done? But here's the thing: when you are doing something that really matters, be all there. For me, any kind of writing – an article, a blog – I turn off the ringer on my phone. I shut down my email. I close Facebook. In doing those simple things, I can usually knock out 500 words – or more - in less than 30 minutes. Part of not multitasking can be using something called "block scheduling." In other words, set time on your calendar

when you will make all of your client calls. Have another block where you will go to networking events. Have a block for administrative tasks. Manage your tasks and your time so you are focusing on the same type of task all at once, which will help you finish more things in a concentrated amount of time.

3. **Manage your energy.** This is about honoring yourself – who you naturally are. If your concentration is at a peak first thing in the morning, then plan your tasks involving concentration then. But if your concentration time is later in the day, or even late at night, don't force yourself to write every morning. Honor your natural rhythm. The same is true for tasks that involve less concentration, and perhaps even more sociability. Plan your networking, coffee meetings, phone calls, and social media time for when you are naturally more open. Managing your energy is also about taking care of yourself well – sleeping, eating nutritious foods, getting some movement in every day, whether it's a walk, yoga or an intense sweat session. Managing your energy is about taking time out as well – a massage, a pedicure, a night out.

4. **Remember:** the way we perceive ourselves is not always how other people perceive us! Do you ever think about all of the words that describe who you are? Business owner? Mom? Creator? Founder? Wife? Partner? Writer? Artist? Dancer? Daughter? Friend? The list can be pretty extensive – and if you stop to really think about it, a teeny bit overwhelming. I

presented at a seminar in June 2014. I had planned a juicy topic involving using the law of attraction to create your ideal life. I opened my sessions with a variation of "what are you hoping to learn today?" Surprisingly, the women asked me how I was able to juggle it all, and accomplish so many things. Well, that wasn't what I planned to talk about – but it was a great lesson in perceptions!

5. **Turn off the phone** when you are working on projects. You are less distracted and your caller gets more of your attention.

6. **Return calls in chunks** with your calendar, pen and paper handy so you can easily make appointments and write things down.

7. **Schedule days in and days out.** In other words, make as many appointments and meetings as possible on as few days as possible so you can focus on desk work on the other days. I typically plan to work at my desk on Monday, Wednesday and Friday afternoons, as well as on Thursday. On Tuesday I spend the day out and about.

8. **Schedule time off.** To take a walk, read a book, paint or whatever your thing is

9. **Work regular hours,** even if you work from home. Use a schedule, even if it is not always 9 – 5! Build in time to take care of yourself and your family.

10. Outsource big things that aren't your expertise. Examples: websites, accounting, bookkeeping, legal.

Don't try to do everything yourself. If you have the choice between spending $100 on child care and $100 on a company that can do what needs done for you, hire the help in your business and enjoy the time with your kids.

11. **Be the face of your business.** You are your own brand. Get to know others and talk about your business. When you are excited, others are excited. Think about why you love what you do.

12. **Set up your time so you have dedicated family time one night a week.** Think Pizza and a Movie, Burgers and Games – something where your whole family can connect. If that doesn't work with work schedules, then aim for a weekend morning to connect over breakfast.

13. **Plan regular family outings or projects**. Whether you are going on a hike or a bike ride, or volunteering at a food pantry, doing something together as a family will bring you closer.

14. **Exercise in the morning.** I know. I'm not always a morning person either, but when you do it in the morning, its done. Your health is important. But its more than that. Exercising early switches on your brain, clearing away any fogginess and helping you to be ready to focus on the rest of your day. You might wonder why you can't exercise later in the day, when you feel more like doing it. You can. I would just encourage you to also spend at least twenty minutes every single morning engaging in some simple form of

movement. Another big reason for planning your exercise first thing is commitment. It is all too easy to have your plan to exercise be curtailed, changed or cancelled if you wait until later in the day. First thing in the morning is your time to plan for yourself. I can already hear an excuse or two.

15. **Watch what you eat, not for your waistline or your health, but for your energy.** If you eat nothing but crap, you will feel like crap. If you eat green things and lean protein, you will have more energy.

16. **Drink water.** The standard advice is to drink eight 8-ounce glasses of water each day. That is the minimum amount of water you should drink. A more realistic number is to drink one-half ounce for every pound you weigh. So if you weigh 200 pounds, you should drink 100 ounces of water each day.

It sounds like a lot, I know. If you aren't a water drinker now, you probably wonder how you will get it all in. So here it is: drink a full glass before you exercise in the morning. Drink another one after you exercise. Put a water container on your desk or nearby during the day. Use a straw – for some reason water seems to go down faster if you use a straw.

17. **Have goals.** Spend the rest of your day accomplishing necessary things. Go to work. Spend time with your kids. Clean your house. And in your free time... pursue a dream. Write a story, paint a picture, pull out the camera and walk into nature snapping whatever you see. Spend time with friends

in a way that doesn't involve food. Open your craft closet and work on your knitting or quilting or needlework. Keep your attention on something you enjoy.

18. **Write down your goals.** 67% of wealthy people write down their goals, only 17% for poor people do. Tom Corley, on his website RichHabits.net.

19. **Review your goals weekly or daily**. Write them down again. It can help to break larger goals into smaller milestones – i.e. if the revenue is $X for the year, then break it down to a $Y for each month. Smaller goals are less daunting – and more attainable. Are you using your time to meet the goals?

20. **Use a calendar.** Have a calendar for your own priorities. And have a large family wall calendar and use it. It helps to keep everyone's information in sight. Some applications allow you to have a shared calendar app on your phone. In some ways, this is a great idea – portable, available. I think it's a good idea to also have the wall calendar, though, because out of sight is out of mind – and if its on the wall it is in your face.

21. **Use block scheduling.** Plan time for quiet desk work, time for calls, time for meetings, time for networking.

22. **Habit and routine will take you a long way.** The more automatic life is, the more energy you have available for the bigger decisions. The less energy you spend on what to eat at a restaurant or what time you

exercise in the morning, the more energy you have to focus on the bigger questions and decisions.

23. **Read**

24. **Use child care.** Whether it is a friend, family member or paid sitter, have a little time away to get things done. Socialization is good for them. Find an evening babysitting service that will allow you to go to mixers or networking events – or just on date nights!

25. **Crockpots.** Crockpots are a busy mom's best friend. You can start a meal in the morning, set the timer and go. A few hours later you have a hot, healthy, delicious meal ready to go. You can even find recipes for "freezer crockpot meals" on the internet. You can prep five or ten meals one afternoon. Freeze everything and just pull out the bag and plop it in the crockpot when you are ready to go.

26. **Make ahead meals.** Freezer meals are another great idea. Again, one afternoon a month you can put together a handful of meals for the family and then put them in the freezer. Some moms will do this in groups – 4 or 5 moms will each bring enough ingredients for their recipe for 20 or 25 people. All of the meals are made, and then each mom takes home enough for her family.

27. **Easy meals.** Have a list – mental or posted on the refrigerator of fast, easy meals that can help you avoid the fast food line or the delivery driver. Some ideas:

- Rotisserie chicken and salad from the salad bar.

- Eggs (eggs and toast, egg sandwiches)

- Grilled cheese and tomato soup

28. **Communicate with your partner about what needs done and who is doing it.** If you keep it going, this doesn't have to be a long or tedious exchange.

29. **Do laundry little by little.** Throw in a load in the morning. Switch it at lunch. Repeat the next day.

30. **Do the dishes when the meal is done.** Yes, the kitchen looks better. Yes, you won't attract bugs. Mainly, though, you won't have this task hanging over your head.

31. **Focus.** For many tasks – try to focus on completely finishing task #1 before starting task #2. This is really hard with kids. You may have pulled the towels out of the dryer, intending to fold them and put them away in the bathroom. In the middle you may be asked for juice, milk, breakfast, clothes and help on the potty. You may remember you need to return a message and help find homework. Wow. Real life. But as much as you can, try to finish the task – so you don't return home hours later to a half-folded pile, just feeling like you still have one more thing to do.

32. **Say no.** Yep. Say no to anything you don't want to do. Don't take on volunteer projects, clients or anything else that you aren't excited about doing. Your priorities are your children, your marriage and yourself. Anything else can take a back seat.

33. **Premade snacks or handy snacks.** I keep cheese sticks and apples in the fridge, along with yogurt, so that the kids always have something they can grab – something I'm okay with them eating several of. Other people put crackers or pretzels or cereal in bags or resealable bowls so the snacks are handy when their hands are otherwise full.

34. **Premade drinks.** One of my friends put a sippie cup of milk in the fridge each night. That way her four year old could get up, get a drink and watch cartoons with his brother for a few minutes, all without waking mommy or interrupting her get ready routine.

35. **Take a few minutes for yourself every day.** Reflect on your goals. Think about what you are doing well.

36. **Be grateful for what you have.** Practice gratitude. Meditation. Prayer. Keep a blessings journal. Focus on the many good things.

37. **Patience.** It takes a lot of patience. Patience with each other, patience with yourself, patience with your children.

38. **Do it now.** If you have a big dream, start it now. We all know people who waiting until. Until the kids grew up. Until the mortgage is paid off. Until. If you have something you are dreaming about, start figuring out how to take small steps towards getting there.

39. **Be in charge of yourself.** Make your own decisions and work with people you want to.

40. **Confidence.** Have confidence that it will work.

41. **Done is better than perfect.** Just put things into action and go.

42. **Know your why.** Find something that makes it worthwhile. Your kids? Your husband? Your vision for how you want your family to work? Know why you work at whatever work you do.

43. **Do something that matters.** If you are not going to be with your kids, then you want to know that you are doing something that matters.

44. **Save.** Save money. Don't spend it all. Have a cushion.

45. **Protect yourself.** Have insurance – life, health, business, home, auto. As much as insurance can cost money, it can also financially protect you in the event of an unplanned disaster. Save your worry energy, and put insurance into place.

46. **Plan meals in advance**. Schedules a week's worth of meals at the beginning of the week and do one store trip for all of the ingredients. Post the menu in the kitchen so you know what you are making for dinner each night. By planning and shopping ahead of time, you know you have everything on hand and she can get it done. It cuts down on the hassle and the headache.

47. **Healthy, quick evening meals**. For a healthy, quick evening meal buy chopped vegetables from the salad bar on the weekend. Add them to part of a bag of lettuce and some grilled chicken or fish for a quick, easy meal. To make it even easier, pick up a pre-cooked rotisserie chicken.

48. **Use PeaPod Grocery delivery.** PeaPod, or another grocery delivery service can save the time and frustration involved in a trip to the store with young children.

49. **Use Amazon Prime**, or other online shopping, for most of your routine purchase.

50. **Be prepared.** Have something ready when the kids come home.

51. **Eat leftovers for lunch.** This is a quick way to have lunch ready for you – whether you are at the office or working from home. Instead of trying to plan lunches and dinners, just make extra at dinner and have the leftovers the next day.

52. **Prepare dinner in advance.** If you work from home, face the reality that if you worked in an office you would take breaks every now and then. While you can't spend the whole day on dishes and laundry, a well-planned fifteen minute break in the early-mid afternoon can give you a change of scenery (and a chance to get over any mid afternoon slump) and can let you prep dinner so it is ready when your spouse walks in the door and the kids are home and everybody is ready to eat. Instead of running around like crazy at dinner, have it ready to go.

53. **Be less perfect.** Do not beat yourself up over being perfect all the time. You can have both. Don't try to be superwoman, to say no is okay.

54. **Your legacy.** You want your kids to remember you as mom. So focus on that -the face time with your kids.

55. **Don't worry about someone else's success.** Focus on your own definition of success and what makes you happy.

56. **Take care of yourself.** Exercise regularly. Do not sacrifice your own health. Eat well, drink water.

57. **Be active.** Use a pedometer or a FitBit to keep track of your activity

58. **Plan your work carefully.** Plan time with your clients, so you know at the beginning of the week days you are spending with the client, what hours, what times, what meetings.

59. **Schedule around client time.** Make client time the first priority during certain hours, and then fill in with your other responsibilities. Do the work that needs to be done.

60. **Family meetings on Sundays.** When your children are little, take this time on Sundays to check in with your spouse about the upcoming week. What big meetings, deadlines, obligations, and desires do you have out there? What is on your spouse's mind? To make a family work well, you want to work together – which starts with communication. As your children are older, have them participate. After all, they have sports and school and homework and music and friends they want to see. It helps the kids to know what's going on with mom and dad – and lets every one work together to make a plan for meeting everyone's needs.

61. **Have dinner at a set time and eat as a family.** This isn't necessarily a productivity tip – but it is a key to staying connected as a family, which is what it is all about for most of us. The idea is that everyone comes back together at the end of the day and talks to each other about our successes, problems, and dreams. Some families do better with breakfast, or an evening snack. The point is to have one set time every day where your family is together, preferably over a meal.

62. **Have a routine**. Kids respond really well to a routine, because they know what's coming next. You never have to alert them to bathtime or bed time. Adults respond pretty well to routines as well.

Routines allow us to do some things by habit – like exercise, drinking our water, or packing a school lunch – so we can focus some of our brain's "deciding" energy on the bigger decisions and problems we are faced with.

63. **Pay attention to your health.** See your doctor regularly. Keep in mind that low physical energy can be a symptom of a number of physical problems, from thyroid deficiency to Vitamin D or magnesium problems. Food and environmental allergies can really impact how motivated you are.

64. **Eat protein**. Anyone who has followed weight loss plans over the last decade or two has heard of the Atkins Plan, the Sugarbusters Plan, and the Zone. One of the primary objectives in all of these plans is to reduce the amount of carbohydrates you eat, increase the amount of protein and thereby allow you to lose fat rapidly. But there are other key benefits to eating enough protein – especially for moms. And they all have to do with energy:

• Protein will keep you full longer, eliminating distractions.

• Protein will help maintain your blood sugar, preventing spikes and dips, allowing you to have constant energy

• Protein controls your appetite and cravings for salty or sweet snacks

• Protein is the primary ingredient your body uses

to make muscle. The movement of muscle burns fat, thus, you want to maintain your muscle.

• Protein is the primary ingredient for many other things in your body – like your skin and your hair. Having an adequate supply will not only help you feel better, but help you look better.

65. **Quick Lunch Tip**. I have a lunch container that I bought at someplace like Target. It has three slots, a large one that takes up just less than fifty percent of the space, and two other spots. If I pack my lunch, I place the protein in the largest spot. If I have a dense protein, i.e. a piece of meat that is as tall as it is wide, I might put it in a smaller spot. I've found that using these containers automatically sizes the portions for me, so that I don't have to think about it – or carry multiple dishes to have my lunch.

66. **Watch your carbs**. This doesn't mean no carbs. It does mean understanding the role carbs play in our body's chemistry – and using that to our advantage to increase our energy and vitality. Lowering carb levels:

• Lowered carb limits will also result in fewer blood sugar spikes

• Carbs are the easiest macronutrient to convert to fat. Limiting the consumption of carbs limits your body's ability to store new fat.

• Reduced carb intake is linked to a flat stomach, and is the best known way to reduce belly fat.

67. **Eat more vegetables and fruits.** This is something everyone says, from your mother to the government. Fruits and vegetables are loaded with vitamins, minerals and antioxidants. They have fiber in them that help keep things moving through your system. You know you need to eat them. One way to add them in to your day is to have a piece of fruit at breakfast and at lunch, and at least two servings of vegetables at lunch or dinner.

68. **Sleep**. While you sleep, your body goes into hibernation. But it also goes into a repair and regenerate mode, turning over skin cells, blood cells and other parts of your body to make you fresh and new. Sleep is also a time when your body resets many of your hormones. If you don't get enough sleep, then your body doesn't reset properly. Sleep. It's good for you.

69. **The Done List**. If you aren't feeling productive, start writing down what you did that day. You will either see that you accomplished a whole lot more than you are giving yourself credit for – or you will see the culprit (Facebook, television,??) staring you in the face.

70. **Priorities and Choices**. Figure out your priorities and then tie how you spend your money and your time back to them. Time and money are the currencies of our lives. And it turns out, you can have it all – it's just about choices.

71. **Dream.** Know what your dream life looks like. Where do you live? Who do you live with? How is It different?

72. **Finish what you start**. Don't be so busy being busy that you don't have time to do things properly. I went through a period of time where I was always forgetting to turn off the lights on my car – resulting in a dead battery every time. Every time I forgot, I was in a huge rush. If I had taken just another 10 seconds before leaving the car each time, I probably would have caught the fact that the lights were on. I would have also saved myself hours of frustration and time, waiting for someone to help jump the battery.

73. **Appreciate the people around you.** As much as our world is crazy busy in the hubbub of life, every time I was "stranded," at least one person stepped up and volunteered to help, without anything more than me asking for help.

74. **Problems can be prevented**. In the law, and in business, it is pretty evident – structure yourself as an LLC or a corporation, use contracts to define parties rights and responsibilities. In life, it can be as simple as remembering that if it is going to be raining, grab your umbrella or raincoat on your way out the door. And of course, in my case, I could take an hour or so to have the right sensor found and replaced at the auto shop.

75. **Automate social media for your business as much as possible**. Use Hootsuite for social media

posting. You can also use Buffer. One of my friends told me a few months ago that I was "everywhere". Really – I'm not. But I do use certain systems to make it look like I am. Some of them – like going to chamber meetings – are just recurring events on my calendar. Others, like posting on social media, is at least 50% owed to the auto posting feature on Hootsuite, which we learned about last month.

76. **Marketing process.** Have a regular, systemized way of keeping in touch with clients and prospects, such as a weekly newsletter.

77. **Contact Management.** Use a CRM or other contact management system to keep track of who you talked to, what you talked about, and when you need to talk to them next. How do you keep track of those leads? Google Mail, Outlook, Task Lists, other programs.

78. **Use your strengths, hire out the rest**. A few months ago, I had one session with a business owner. He was a skilled and talented person, with years of mechanical experience – and he had little business experience. He was very literally learning as he went. He had even hired a few people to help show him the ropes, but he frustrated because the help he really needed wasn't being provided. We went through some really basic things about running a business – from using contracts to protect yourself, to delegating some of your work (like bookkeeping and answering the phone). He and I run into each other regularly and he has said, more than once, that the plan we came up

with together has taken a load off of his shoulders and helped him focus his energy on his strengths.

79. **If you're stuck, where are you stuck?** I recently worked with a client on a project. She knew for months that she wanted to complete this project in her business, and she had no idea about where to even start. She felt stuck in the situation she was in – and stuck on how to move forward. We met several times to discuss her project, and her ultimate goals. Working together, we outlined all of the steps she needed to take on the project – from start to finish. We then went through and talked about assigning those tasks. More than half of what was on the list were things she couldn't – or didn't want – to do herself. We were able to come up with a half a dozen resources for her to contact to get more of the list done. She's not quite finished right now – but she is very clear on what she needs to do to make her dream happen.

80. **DELEGATE** (accounting, bookkeeping, answering the phone, web work, logo design, data entry). Vas are plentiful and out there. If there is something you don't like doing or you know is not your strength, find someone who can help with it. In terms of hiring a VA, my best tip is to ask other business owners who they use. Randomly finding one is taking a chance you may not be able to afford. "But it's just me," is something I've heard in response to "Delegate." That's okay. You can still delegate. In this day of mushrooming small businesses, there is likely a company out there that you can outsource your tasks

to. I use one company for event planning, another for graphic design and marketing services and a third to answer the phones and schedule appointments. All of this lets me focus on the important things for my work: meeting with clients and preparing their custom solutions.

81. **Use contracts in your business**. They protect you and they protect the client. Contracts are valuable because they define who is responsible for what. They make very clear where the money is coming from, where the effort is coming from, and what the time frame is.

Contracts can be oral or written – but it is easier to enforce them if they are written. Contracts are used for services, goods, property – basically any business transaction. Some essential elements: Party A, Party B, Scope – what work is going to be done?, Money / Consideration – who is paying whom, Timeframe – when will the work be done.

Granted, many of the contracts I write include a number of other clauses, including the confidential nature of information, where any law suit would be litigated, and collections and attorneys fees clauses --- but the basic parts are most important – who is doing what for whom for what amount of money in what timeframe? You should have a system for contracts – or agreements – or purchase orders – so that you treat the customer's request for your goods or services the same way every time.

82. **Create and use checklists.** Getting the work done with checklists happens at small three-man business and at large corporations with thousands of employees. Its not just about the work itself, its also about all of the systems that support the work of the business: accounting, HR, payroll.

83. **Time management and the phone.** Be unavailable by phone for certain hours of the day. Return calls in blocks. Use phone unavailable time to complete big projects with more focus.

84. **Have a business number.** An easy way for a solopreneur to have a business number is to use Google voice. Google will allow anyone with a gmail account to have a Google number. You can forward (or port) this number anywhere – and you can choose when it is answered or when it goes directly to voice mail. This has been very handy for me in business because I can forward my number to an answering service. I can decide what hours the service answers the phone. And I can stop people from calling my direct line at any hour of the day and night. Google Voice sends you a message (voice to text) of who called and why, so if you are inclined you can call back right away – but if you are trying to unplug and pay attention to the person in front of you, you can "ignore" the business calls without having to put your cell on silent.

85. **Time block appointments.** Try to have appointments reasonably back to back so you can focus on your appointments and don't waste time feeling like there's not enough time to "get anything done." At the same time, schedule enough time between appointments and meetings so that you aren't rushed.

86. **Use one calendar that is accessible everywhere.** Google Calendar can be accessed on the computer, your smart phone and your tablet. Most applications will sync with this calendar as well. If you enter all of your appointments in one spot, you will have a better chance of keeping track of them. It makes scheduling and planning really easy. I can also share it with select people (like my husband) so that he knows what's going on with me and can schedule things for both of us – or just find out why I am not answering his call.

87. **For intense projects, schedule the time to complete them on the calendar in one big block**. We all have those things that just need an hour or four to finish. We can be much more productive at finishing them if we sit down to do these things all in one block of time, rather than starting and stopping multiple times throughout the day. So if you have a big task to work on, schedule the time on your calendar. It will prevent you from scheduling meetings and appointments in the middle of that time and reserve that block for uninterrupted work.

88. **Keep a task list.** We all have a hundred seemingly mundane things to do. Return a phone call, send an email, make a copy, put that piece of paper in the file. If you aren't careful, something can get lost in the shuffle. Keeping a list – whether as a task list in Google tasks or in Outlook, or just on an old fashioned piece of paper – can prevent those things from getting lost. Use Google tasks if you are a Google user.

89. **Use mobile technology**, but only use it during your downtime – don't fiddle with it around potential clients and referral partners

90. **Create your own luck**. One of my favorite quotes: Luck is when preparation meets opportunity. I think you create your own luck. It's easy, isn't it, when we are the business owner or the manager or the professional, to take all of the glory when things go right. I thought of that idea. I implemented that successful program. I did that. But when things don't go according to plan, it's not nearly as fun. This is when the blame game is likely to happen. Who missed something? Who didn't follow through? It's not nearly as easy to look in the mirror and realize that our own successes and failures start with us. It's also hard in the middle of the "failure" to realize that oftentimes, our greatest lessons are hidden inside of our failures. I'll give you full disclosure. I have made mistakes – some of them big. I have made decisions that I have regretted. But when I reflect back, those bad decisions and big mistakes ended up being the foundation for something fantastic. Sao go out there and be fantastic. You never know when your

preparation will meet your opportunity and create your lucky day.

91. **Breathe. Play. Read. Dream**.

92. **Don't stop learning**. Be open to new ideas and new ways of accomplishing things.

93. **Don't wait to follow your dreams.**

BOOK BONUS

There is even more helpful information, tips and tricks available online.

Go to http://kathycatlindavis.com/?page_id=1582 to sign up for the bonus content. You can also sign up for the weekly newsletter, read the blog and find out all sorts of new ideas to try.

THE CONTRIBUTORS

This book was made possible in part thanks to some incredible women who took the time to talk with me about their struggles, successes and solutions in balancing a business and a family.

Natalie Rose, Rose Promotions and Common Sense Bookkeeping

Natalie is the owner of Common Sense Bookkeeping since the spring of 2012 and Rose Promotions since the fall of 2012. She co-owns Rose Promotions with her husband Brian and she is the sole owner of Common Sense Bookkeeping.

"I think that the important thing is focusing on the future. One of the big benefits is that pride and accomplishment that you are doing it not just because you are doing it, but you are doing it for yourself. It is a big reason to get out of the bed in morning and get going."

Natalie most enjoys small businesses generate ideas on how to improve their business.

Natalie is a graduate of Marian College. She and her husband have two young children.

Susan Young, Aim Fire Marketing

Susan is the owner of AimFire Marketing, an Indianapolis area marketing consultancy specializing in writing for online and offline marketing (since 2005). She works primarily with small businesses who need a reliable, professional and outsourced marketing resource to support the sales effort.

Susan has more than 15 years of experience in various marketing communications roles, from corporate marketing to agencies, and have worked in the Indianapolis market since 2001. Her experience spans many industries, from high-tech to financial services, life sciences and retail.

Susan holds a Bachelor of Science degree in Advertising from the University of Illinois at Urbana-Champaign.

Susan and her husband have two children.

Jessica Brockway, Accounting Solutions Plus

Jessica is the owner of Accounting Solutions Plus, a firm that offers complete accounting and business management services. Her business is a voice for her clients. Her goal is to help her client's businesses succeed.

"Owning your business and working from home gives you more pros than cons. I have the flexibility to be the mom I want to be. "

Jessica holds a Bachelor of Science in Accounting and Business Management from Kaplan University.

Jessica is married, and has three children, all boys. They are eleven, eight and a half and two.

Sheryl Matthys, Successful Women Made Here.

Sheryl launched "Successful Women Made Here" as a place for women to discover what they really want and how to make it happen as entrepreneurs, and/or working moms for their business, relationships, and their families.

Throughout her career, Sheryl served in front and behind the camera. She's a best selling author, TV/radio host and guest expert, news reporter, actress for TV & voiceover commercials, website entrepreneur, producer of a TV pilot and documentary, and professor at the University of Notre Dame, St. Mary's, and Indiana University-SB. Sheryl's attracted the media attention of Fox & Friends, E!, Bravo, ABC News Now, Sirius/XM, The New York Times, Wall St. Journal, USA Today, and others. Sheryl is also a columnist for FIDO Friendly magazine.

Sheryl is the mother of 2 young children and has lived in New York, California, Indiana, Kentucky, and Paris, France.

ABOUT THE AUTHOR

Kathy Catlin Davis

Kathy is the owner of KJD Legal, a virtual law firm dedicated to helping entrepreneurs and professionals start, own and operate the business they have been dreaming of. From establishment to contracts, trademarks to copyrights, Kathy helps businesses protect what's theirs and sleep easily at night.

Kathy holds a Bachelor of Arts from Indiana University in Bloomington, and a Juris Doctor from Indiana University School of Law Indianapolis. Kathy is licensed to practice law in the States of Indiana and Florida.

Kathy and her husband, Jim, have two boys, John and Kaden, who specialize in getting dirty and climbing on things.

Kathy Catlin Davis

www.ingramcontent.com/pod-product-compliance
Lightning Source LLC
Chambersburg PA
CBHW021446170526
45164CB00001B/409